ACKNOWLEDGEMENTS

Lapwing Publications gratefully acknowledges the permission of Blackstaff Press to publish these poems, some of which appear in "Ruined Pages" their recently published collection of Padraic Fiacc's work, some of which appear as variants of the same texts. Lapwing also acknowledges the many publications in which some of these poems first appeared.

Lapwing Publications gratefully acknowledge the financial assistance of the **Arts Council of Northern Ireland** and **The UK Foundation for Sport and the Arts** in the publication of this pamphlet.

PUBLISHED BY
LAPWING PUBLICATIONS
c/o DENNIS & RENE GREIG
1 BALLYSILLAN DRIVE
BELFAST BT14 8HQ

TYPESET BY
LAPWING GRAFIX
c/o BRIAN CHRISTIE
51 KILCOOLE GDNS
TELE: 712483

PRINTED BY TEXTFLOW SERVICES LTD
SCIENCE LIBRARY, MALONE ROAD BELFAST
TEL: 663591

ISBN 1 898472 08 4

LAPWING POETRY PAMPHLET
PADRIAC FIACC: WOE TO THE BOY
PUBLISHED 1994

CONTENTS

**TO MARY DENVIR,
OF BOOKFINDERS**

SAINT BRIGID'S DAY

(for Christopher Kelly)

Sheep milk time is come.

The branch snows
From stem of seedful sap,
Ripens raiding shooting light
Sends the wry-neck back.

'Quick, Quick' it sings

Wrenching a head around
Against the blight
Winter left in worms
For eating things.

The nightingale
Sings all
The morning now.
The green woodpecker
                    laughs
'Ha Ha Hello'.

A WONDER
(for Darragh)

A salmon smoke comes up out of dead sun
Every spring after the rains of May
When school-bored boys trudge dreamily to school.

The new-flamed roots are on their secret run
And weave with thousand spider legs the way
Of things that dream, that sit upon a stool

And write the alphabet in Greek in scunder
Upon the slates of beating rote.
                                        I wonder.

I wonder will the blue jay fly low down
Out of a thousand clouds I love from look
Up all at once out of the history book

And perch itself right on the window-sill?
In this school-tower up above the town
I am too near to sky to use 'strong will'.

Outgrowing countrymen ten hills below
The sky comes round my cranium (lets in through).

My granda does not know all that I know.

THE STOLEN FIFER

I was brought up in a rampart
On top of a slieve where the heart
Had its wine fill of beauty once.
I was brought up in a trance.

I was brought up in a tower.
I was brought up with the poor and the done
Old man so that the Wind of the Sid̄
Did not find it hard on its power
To weave the Web of Dream over me.

Now I am locked in the dūn
And the people of wing and of wind and of wine
Sing to me at the rise of the moon
And sing to me till the last star shine.

And I am a boy forever from growing
And I am a man forever from sowing
And no man knows what I be knowing
When wind is on the pine and blowing.

I was brought up on top of a slieve
And cannot live on the earth, for the town
Of the earth which I do not believe
In, pulls me down, pulls me down.

STORM BIRD

My comings and goings
Are the comings and goings of wind.

I am the word that the wind mutters.
Pay me no mind.

Though I serve beauty and not mankind
The voice is the bird of a word
Wind gives wings to.

I am the blackbird
Of the ruined nest who sings

'All is beauty to the blind.'

JACKDAW
(for John Hewitt)

On Carnlough sand look up to sky
And let the waves come into beach.
The terrible great flying down of winds screech
That storm is good.

I am a jackdaw, and I am shrewd
And I have flown from beach to wood
And back again.

And I have nested in a tower
In hollow oaks and rabbit burrow
And in crevices of cliffs here.

So should you ask me, then,
I who have known flower,
I who have known furrow,
I who have known tear,

I who have built sticks of straw
Of nest-lost and my own feather,
I who have tasted law
I who have tasted weather.....

Should you ask me, should
I would say yes, and caw
That storm is good.

A WANT IN ME
(for Joe O'Connor)

Sweet little seconds watching the ugly gull
I spend holding a head up dreaming up
Into the loneliness of the skies.

I stick my tongue out at the powerful.
No arm of a strong man can break what I build up
And I do not care about the wise.

I have no set-purpose in the whole wide world.
Nothing that the world can give me can please me for long.
I close my eyes to the moment that passes.

Nor am I right enough to love the furled
Flag on the responsible street. The fife, the song
Only I love, and the clouds, and the grasses.

THE POET

(for Padraig O Snodaigh)

I am the chaunt-rann of a Singer
Who has sung to heart at night
How the rust-loch's hazel waters
Mirror the stars all right:
Christ on a tree for you and me
And the moon-dark worlds between!

I am the chaunt-rann of a Singer
Who has sung to heart by day
How the grey rain on the wet street
Washes our lives away:
Christ on a tree for you and me
And the sun-bright worlds between!

I am the chaunt-rann of a Singer
Who does not cease chaunt with loam
As the crouched lime of the good earth
Eats us away on home:
Christ on a tree for you and me
And none of the worlds between!

MAKING POEMS

(for Conleth Ellis)

Hermit on sand weaving straw
Baskets I cast to the wave's
Maw what I finish then
Weave another out in
Penny-wise sea wind

The same childhood at the end
Of the road as at the beginning

The same hieroglyphic bird word

Fish of the sea my work is for you
I made this poem for a thing to do

That it may tickle a salmon throat
That an empty sea shell ear
Hear its bell-tone note:

The laugh-cry of some journey man
Building mud towers in the sand!

(Yes see how they shake and slant

Waiting for the waves to break
Their imperfection and their want.)

STOLEN CHILD

(for Michael Longley)

'From a world more full of weeping than you can understand.' W. B. Yeats.

You watch us guide our paper boat
Across a brick-yellow flood
Cement-dusted summer's hole
In the New Town Road
Has you standing up leaning
Too far over the one side....

Your tiny heart-sick head pops
Brooding ears, perched not
Far from grunt of hanging cloud!

Heart-frightened wings
Thrash dreaded water;
The swan-hungering-bread air!
(A creature you alone can hear
Hiss at your barren eyes)

Shining like honey, the bees
Cultivated in abandon, forgot
The hive-home, a toad
Sitting on the top
Gulping down each one!

Your head is a staid dawn
Will moon not, will never know
Night but child-stay the sandy
Linnet of a winter's day.

SURETY

(for Carl Louis Baker age three)

In the Black Loch where
The herring gull
Hangs hovering over
The treasure and skull
The small boys swim

And laugh in their play
And all bad pull
In the veins of the limb
of some Fionn can stay
At the bottom of the water

For the mad dark day
Of Cormac's daughter
Passes away
That the children still
(Tho' men still kill)

The children still
In this evil day
Wade in the water
And dance and play.

SEED
(for Anthony Weir)

By the Bath House where North Man
Thinned flesh by flogging leaf
To the burn of steaming wind
Seared petulant body brawn to bone

(Borne in the end by time, the thief
Far from Cahon's Tirkane)
Not a German Greek but out of mind
The slimy stone, the moss remain
And here and there in Maghera:
the cinder

A small brick-haired boy whose ancestor
Was some orange Dane
Cannot yet say 'Da'
Answers back the centuries 'Yes Sir!'

Strays near the Great Wall in witless disdain
Tramps barefoot on the skull of the charred emperor
Darts back up the blind back street
The autumn coloured clouds his bedtime store

Himself the living trophy left
Of all that red gold gore.

CHILDREN AT PLAY IN THE BOTANIC GARDEN

(for Laura Martina Victoria Hyde age 2)

There is beneath sea-wind a by-path where
Foxes evade the dawn and young fawns tarry
Where the vines of the ever-grape,
still hanging there
Go unspoiled, uncrunched, unmade
into wine.
Young children, for all I care, still carry
Away the store of berry from the
ever-vine.
Here they will grow up, and bloom
and become and marry
And beget, and die, and still, that
by-path mine
By right of remembering only, is open
only
To them to spoil if they like, but they
will not, they make sweet
Under the twigs and laurels the thole
of the lonely
As they beat down the dust of the world
with their dancing feet.

SAINT PATRICK TURNS THE SOD
(for Leland Bardwell)

Gold as a sun through a wine from pears
Is the glass moon in a spring wind
Sheds tears
On red-haired rusted willow.

An unremitting green
Scars of the ground sing
Clouds in torrents, then
A thousand stars
Waken the birds and the children.

Transparent through the leaf, the wing,
The blackbirds in the drying silence
sing
All at once light on the ice-broken river!

A lyric myriad of wild swans
Arch to be flying...

The earth is aired with bits of bone
And will not stiffen

Thanks be to the worm.

LEGEND OF THE SOWER OF THE SEAS

The mighty Muiridach of Carn
King-son, lord that he was
Listened to his lectures
As the head-bowed student does.

From Achad-abhla's site
He then set up Carlow
And for seven years taught love
With a voice deep and slow.

Then anon, he built
Clonard's proud rampart
And nursed the strong man there
With masterly human heart.

The Colmcille, the Canice
The Brendans sailed from here
The multitudes of scholars
Splitting hair from hair.

From Gildas and David and Cadoc
From Fortkern of Roscor
Strode with a burning nature
Saint Finnian, the Day Star.

LEGEND OF THE SPRING FINDER

I am Rory's son, Conn's friend to God
And king-son Conor on Connacht's sea
And Connacht's fog-drunken hilly lands
All bow low to me.

God makes the moon move when I move.
I am king-son and king
And my soul is a storm-green morning
To which angels sing.

My hands will bring forth of earth.
I and breaking waters are one.
Conor nourishes the ground
Being Rory's son.

THE BEGINNING OF THE STORMS
(Oiśin Sings)

Fionn in Norway came on
A sparrowy black pea cock
Tame as a pet, bold as a boy's son
Swinging over the Loch
A woodlark at Sowan

Provoking appetite by dance of the beak,
Gold, upturned.
The warble of the note
Subtle to no knowing ear
Reaching, for the size of the throat

The wide carrying-over fjord-horizon
A song without word.
The bird was human but,
Clever, Fionn said, alert to his summon.
He swore it could hear and understand

Finding no thing in the world 'queer'
Going into the hero's hand
As into his own due.
I tell you, Patrick
That is why there are blackbirds in Ireland

Here in Derry Cairn
Swarming over, shadowing
Storm-lit Loch Erne.
Fionn brought the creature here
Started the swarm.

TENTH CENTURY INVASION

(for Tina Kelly)

Doves beat their wings
Against their breasts...
Bloodying their wings
Bloodying their breasts...

Bells ring throughout
                    the book
At the bottom of the Loch:
Gold running over the
                ruined page

Drowned
Emerald and lilac ink
From the song written in
The shaft of the sun
In the moment on the
                        margin
Never to be sung.

OLD POET
(for Padraic Colum)

Strong as the seedling the clay -
Reared winging bird, bald
But not bent head
The snow thawed on
A yellowing lead from time
(Rattled the lift he took
At night fornenst the park
As time as blood ran
Coming home in the dark)
Sings still the single word:

The workhouse and the road
The turf bog, the poplar in Mullingar,
The furze bold as flesh,
The heather weather as blood
The grain from the corn,
The trampling thresh of existence-limited feet
The vision of futility
As if it did not matter what
It is better not to be than born.

The pines stood up as guests about the Hundred and First
Street Lake,
A table of frozen black glass.
He waved a hand up to the copper beech
To let the grey-faced student strolling with him
A tworthree bit of say.

Arguing about El Greco and de Valera
The eye more on the sparrow than the ear on his own
word
Who strolled the streets of Dublin with James Joyce
And had, like the rest, a bit of tiff with Yeats...

Under the iced branches of Central Park West
With a voice could be Daniel Corkery
Said what Yeats said, what the best said
'Dig in the garden of Ireland, write of your own.'

When we came to Ninety Sixth Street he
Flung eyes over the old roads
Of the Midlands still looking home,
Blotted out a penthouse here to scan a hill there
Skimmed the snow on the grass as a boy-thrown stone
Skies the skin of water shyfully...

As seasons, passing, the rain
Left on the pavements where the pigeons are
The dead leaves of a summer sun...

Wind, a wren-wrought silk-for-nesting web
Closed over the havocked to ivory grass.
Smoked ravens with chimneys drifted
Filtered past hunched back silent cats of years
On a wash-line left hanging
Open gates: Unripened
Waiting, crude grain, raw

In the wood, still thriving from
Fermenting childhood's thinning comb
Of wine in time ripening
Truth, a beauty, and a good
Hive-sieve for man, the bee:

His wounds, birdmade, feet-pecked, scar-crowed,
Grin with beaks of panicking gold,
The shuddering wing gasping against the bar of the human
Hand touching the butterfly but not to death
With a green thumb forefinger clutch,
The touch of a mother of a woman

In a lifetime of peace, betrayed or told as a song
The moss winning left on the log,
He girds up his loins and laughs
At the buried bone dug up by the dog
At life, toothless toward night fall.

LEGEND OF THE SUNKEN CATHEDRAL

I flew over the Donkey's Village.
I laughed to Brother Wind's hand.
Moving privately, I confessed.
He sent me to the Strand...

'Your penance, my son, the blackbird
Is to fly to the raw, strange sea
And to mutter a prayer on cathedral wood
With a prayer there for me.'

I flew to the cross in whiteness
To sing to Christ a hundred prayers
And lost was the day for its brightness
And many were the murky airs.

But slowly the land gave way to the sea
O the raw, strange sea. O the raw, strange sea.
And quickly the wrath of its rawness was free.
O the raw, strange sea. O the raw, strange sea.

And it spat and creeped and gurgled its way
And the red stained glass was swallowed in grey.
Said the sea to the saint 'Come Away. Come away.
Come Away...Away...Come Away...Away.'

WINTER ON HIS BRIDE TO BE SPRING A CHILD

(for Aine)

Fionn sings

The hair a fair May Day.
Eyes, sunlit pear leaves.
Two moons over the tiny mouth
The star-green eyes!

The mouth:
A little valley to the south.

She tosses child-hair over from
her eyes:
Leaves of the copper pear-tree
gleam.
Grainne, daughter of the House
of Art

Is granted me
As sky grants the ground
The fall of the hawthorn flower
The seed-bearing gold bee
The brilliant red holly bird.

Two eyes are morning heather
Star-green at moon light.

The small mouth
Looks but an eye away
From my beard,
as if in flight!

THE BURNING GARDEN

1.

Ghostly asters blow
To such a dusky
Sinking
The whole slow
Day, least for long
As gold body burns,
Then greys
That summer seems long,
Long when you are young
And in the oven
Waiting to glaze.

2.

She lit queer rushes of her eyes
And blew out all around.
I swear sheer fire sank sea-wise
Into dead ground.

The reverie I'm left of her
Flares up gorse-whin lit
Pine cone stars behind the fir:
The like of it

Did not end before I'd moan
'My days be what you bid!'
(I did not know she could have flown)
But since she flit

I cultivate bird clay, I save
A true illusion grows
Beyond all burning that a brave
Body does.

That no one passes
Through the grave
But we still love.

DERANGED

Liefer would I turn and love
The ox in the bypath, the sloe on the bush
Than take to the blithe creature would crush
All in her hands!

It is fitting not for a young man
To turning of face backward like this
Carrying a cut from the knife of her kiss,
The smart of her lips!

O comely indeed the arrangement of her hair!
Beyond that the ease of her shoulder,
Her two blue eyes: nothing colder!
Her two blue eyes!

O moonlight that wasted me, O harsh little stars:
Sharp cutting reproaches from what tongue could not say!
She left me alone one scald of a day,
The deceit of the one!

Liefer would I turn and love
The ox in the bypath, the barn-yard dove!

THE BOY AND THE GEESE

(for Brigid)

The swans rise up with their wings in day
And they fly to the sky like the clouds away

Yet with all their beauty and grace and might
I would rather have geese for their less-smooth flight.

I would rather have geese for they're ugly like me
And because they are ugly, as ugly can be

I would rather have geese for their mystery.

ALIVE ALIVE O

The altar boy from a Mass for the dead
Romps through the streets of the town
Lolls on brick studded grass
Jumps up, bolts back down
With wild pup eyes...

This morning at twist of winter to spring
Small hands clutched a big brass cross
Followed the stern brow of the priest
Encircle the man in the box...

A bell-tossed head sneezed
In a blue daze of incense on
Shrivelled bit lips, then
Just to stay awake, prayed
Too loud for the man to be at rest...

O now where has he got to
But climbed an apple tree!

AFTER THE STORM

Wrecked white lupins
To sods crack the young
Red boughs still
With gold buds.

The pink ash
Of a fire-dead
Corn-flower sky
Has no wing left
To ring us a tune

In slime now with
Moss on the stone
Is the cloud over
The face of
The brown moon!

O redwinged blackbird
Without your worm
What do you do
Where do you go
After the storm?

MAN ALIVE

The beggarman playing a saw
In the arcade
Is blind and dumb
Has one leg
While they who drop pennies
                                        into his cap
Have nothing to see
Have nothing to say
And with their two legs
Where do they go
Where do they come from
Where do they meet?

The crowd is no one nowhere.

I, the blind, the dumb,
                                the crippled beggarman

Am some one
And I am here
Making music.

Everyday I hear a cry of despair
A voice of the defeated
As they drop pennies into my cap.

Everyday I hear my own self
Making music.

MASTER CLAY

On top of the mountain, the school,
                                        a monastery...
I take the road up to the bells.
(The bells are a childhood memory!)

Monks are at prayer. Birds at laughter.
Bells peal in still blue air.

I am afraid of the wall of woods though
Afraid of the sea below, the shadow:
(Lest I fall!)
                        'Come back down, you!'
Waves roar in blackening sky
'You will die for you carry your grave with you
And many's the worm!' I settle in my little cell.
It is not home: Sea wind
Comes in cracks in my skull...
I climbed the whole way up the mountain to
An open wound rooted in the dead
In the ground is my very own
Clump of slime-green clay

Might not have ever been or
Having been is now but more!

THEME FROM A GLOSS

(for Tom and Bernie)

The mountain wall a roof
Higher than waves
Houses tall

Overhead over the book
Shadows
Of sea-wood dippers fall

Wing on wing on wing;
I cannot use my head at all

To copy psalms
With psalms
The water ousel sings...

'Book in hand under
Wing-flowering oak
I learn better here
Than stuck at the school
Of auburn hair
Ablaze at her move.'

I write.
        The cuckoo above
(By the way he can read)
Drops lime on the page
Cuckoos with me.

LUCK

(after the Irish of Donnchadh Mor O Dalaigh for Dennis and Rene)

A green breasted tit-wit
By cool of the shore hops:
The wren, my favourite

Makes nest in the rinsed yew
A trim basket hat lets
The rain through...

The jaw and chirp on him
You would think our man
Is on great foray
With big doom

The brood and himself gathered to eat
Grub trapped between
Tittering feet.

A drop of rain would drown
The family of them.

To think the lapwing plover
Of crest and crown
Is rendered chickless
The stone-built nest
Knocked down

When the wren's whole dozen
Neath an oak leaf
Is spared the storm, my own
And the plover's grief!

DIRGE

(for Ben Alexander Simmons aged five)

Against the down twilighting
I came on my gold bee's
Fur-sheen burnt black
Gold gone rust between
Bars where wings once were
On the little fellow's back.

I made this shelter for
Creatures to be in
Drinking honey and planting
Sea-green clover.
Who killed my brazen pet
Every bold flower's boy-lover?

Ancient sages would find
This a danger sign
A plague's beginning
Would take cover
Down under the earth and
Drown themselves in wine!

TRYING TO STUDY PHILOSOPHY

(for Esmond Birnie)

It's long the love
Song the black
Bird's orange bill

Warbles down
Belfast Loch
Eleven centuries

That it can still
Enamour the seed
In you!
        O ever-
Living,
        little
Black bell

What is 'beautiful'?
What is 'true'?

NORTH MAN
(for Michael McLaverty)

Silent the river red in the snow,
In faltering twilight year after year
A lifting wind falls:
The red sun is down, the swans disappear.

Along the evening Lagan we
Walking the broken dream under the bent bough,
Stop to adhere to the birds,
Known and named, as if by Adam, by you,
Creating poetry without words
Building silence like a house.

I recall yourself and the birds
In tune with the sky gone down.

We walked with silence as if on a dream.
You spoke in the end as if on wind
But how far were your words flung like seed
Over stone

'Passionate and dense as the half-said thing'

Hungering like the teeth of the sea?

Belfast 1947

AIR LETTER FROM MICHAEL McLAVERTY

Yourself the boy you're master to
You wrote
'The young lark not able
To manipulate her throat
-ful of note'

That in Strangford still
An East Wind would make
The women be 'cross as sharks' or

Lightening'd by the window's blink
Of a snicker of sun
The whole school feasting at
A shining in the dark
Delph-glinting sky
                                        Sea-roar
-Wingings stir with your word
And even
            the silent, secret, shy,
(Song heard only when they fly,)
Sea lark sings...

Manhattan 1952

LAMENT FOR THE BARD

(for the Family Sibelius 1956)

The giant traveller stayed
In his own land to hear
Each leaf stir

First theme, first
Movement of his second in D
Is flown down gone
And the stars over
        the thousand
Lakes, lit
with the mid-night sun on
The tree-house at Jar
-Venpaa glow
With morning as in
The opening wood wind
Sorrow, a swan, sets
Her head inside her wing...

STUDENT DESCENDING

Slipping out the door back to
A poor man's schooling world
I study barbed wire sleet
Slashes the mountain-hill wall
An ice-lit cliff to bull
                    feet
Slide back under them

I shudder and slough off
                    the wolf
Goat self before he
Owl-hoot a gull-caw
Sea-crow, of root-flight,
Study, and but for all that
Do not know much more
Only like leap, leap
All the way back down to
Bullets starring the
          dark like fire-flies
Goodbye blue heather
        and forget-me-nots.

Calicoon l945

AT AUTUMN BIRDS OF PASSAGE
(for Aoife Mac Poilin)

A poem is a prayer - Samuel Becket

Stay with us earth smell of air
And steam of dung,

Stay with us stint birds
Who make us dream
Of where you're from.

Bring back the bone-buried
Dog-eared old shoe
                    of the heart
And out of it make
(Out of a sow's lug)
A work here and there
Of ground-hollow art

And bridle, bridle the teeth
Of brutal night life with
The bit of love.